#LLF The Movement

Twelve Life Hacks for Teenagers
to Live Life Fully

TAMSYN ROSE

BALBOA.
PRESS

A DIVISION OF HAY HOUSE

Balboa Press books may be ordered through booksellers or by contacting:

Balboa Press
A Division of Hay House
1663 Liberty Drive
Bloomington, IN 47403
www.balboapress.com.au
1 (877) 407-4847

Because of the dynamic nature of the Internet, any web addresses or links contained in this book may have changed since publication and may no longer be valid. The views expressed in this work are solely those of the author and do not necessarily reflect the views of the publisher, and the publisher hereby disclaims any names and personal details have been changed to protect privacy.

The author of this book does not dispense medical advice or prescribe the use of any technique as a form of treatment for physical, emotional, or medical problems without the advice of a physician, either directly or indirectly. The intent of the author is only to offer information of a general nature to help you in your quest for emotional and mental well-being. In the event you use any of the information in this book for yourself, which is your constitutional right, the author and the publisher assume no responsibility for your actions.

Any people depicted in stock imagery provided by Thinkstock are models, and such images are being used for illustrative purposes only. Certain stock imagery © Thinkstock.

Print information available on the last page.

ISBN: 978-1-5043-0438-2 (sc)
ISBN: 978-1-5043-0439-9 (e)

Balboa Press rev. date: 10/13/2016

Dedication: To my greatest teachers; my family with love always xo

Contents

The LLF Revolution

Hey guys,

I'm so glad you found this book. It means it's your time for emotional evolution and everything is about to change.

LLF stands for Live Life Fully. This is not just a book, but a movement for *real* and *lasting change*, a step-by-step hack to life. So pay attention. These are powerful teachings that encourage you to achieve your full potential. Strap yourself in because you are joining a Revolution.

You will learn how to;

- Get more of what you want
- Deal with every emotion and make it a strength
- Control your sabotaging patterns that keep messing things up
- Heal from the past and really move on
- Control your thoughts and beliefs and get them on your side
- Forgive anything
- Communicate to resolve stuff permanently
- Create a life you are excited to live

The world is changing and the future is uncertain. This is creating a wave of anxiety unlike any other time. More than ever, you must learn how to access your ability to master your emotions, thoughts and beliefs. Rather than being controlled and dragged around by the ups and downs of life, you can learn to make these changes work to your advantage. Changing the world around you, must begin with you.

No matter how you got here, I wrote this book for you. No matter how bad, or hopeless it might feel now, you can become free of the labels and beliefs that hold you back. You can start again, but only if you grab this opportunity with both hands.

There is no better feeling than living your life's purpose. To discover this you need to let go of what limits you. These are the things that get you down or mad, and take the wind out of your sails. I promise you can change your life. The secret is the more you put into this, the more you will get out of it, and this is all up to you.

I want you to remember that growth is uncomfortable and change can feel strange. It can trigger all kinds of feelings. Change is what we are here for, so remember it is a good thing. Don't avoid those uncomfortable feelings. Let them happen.

Be greedy and grab all the tools on offer. Even if you choose not to use some of them now, they will be there for you when you need them. Make a commitment to yourself to finish this book. Consider it an adventure as you discover what you get out of the entire experience.

You might be wondering why you should listen to anything I have to say, you don't know me, and I haven't proven myself to you. I haven't had the toughest life. But I've had a little of everything. I've had my fair share of loss, pain, trials, some amazing opportunities and adventures. All of these experiences have taught me something. I believe in making the most of whatever comes my way. My aim is to share with you the best of what I've learned so you can take the short cut. Allow me to introduce myself a little.

I was born in England into a simple country life. I loved being around animals in the fresh air and growing veggies with Gran. My family had it's own set of problems. I grew up with stories of bad choices, fighting, divorce, and secrets where no one knows the truth anymore. Some of these stories I remember and some visit my nightmares from time to time. Many of them are just a part of my history.

You have your own key moments in life. These are the experiences that shape you and spin your course in different directions. Your story is simply what happened to you. It doesn't limit you or your future, unless you let it. Your experience in life can shape you, but it does not need to define you.

Sometimes things in my life's story are painful. I imagine these feelings and memories sit stored in some invisible box, in the back of my mind, for me to pull out and clear when I'm ready. Some people call this Pandora's Box, I'm going to call it "my little box of stuff". It's important to remember everyone has their stuff, and everyone will find their own way to deal.

No matter what you have locked in your "little box of stuff", you can have a totally fresh start - no exceptions. I will show you step-by-step how to work through it, finally resolve and finish with it. You will then be free to move on and discover who you are. This is everything you need to Live your Life Fully. This revolution for change all starts with you.

Deep breath… Now Leap...

Love Tam xo

Why Me?

Let's start here – why you? You may be wondering what all this has to do with you? How can this help you, or why you should experiment with the tools in this book? Let's start by taking a quick look at how you have been feeling.

Below is a simple self-assessment to evaluate your current emotional state and sense of happiness in your life. Answer the questions honestly based on how you feel most of the time, especially over the last couple of weeks:

Depression, Anxiety and Stress Scale (DASS21) Adapted:

For each statement below, please circle the number in the column that best

	How true is this for you in the last 2 weeks	Not at all	Some times	Quite	Most of the time
O	I found it hard to unwind	0	1	2	3
□	I felt I had a really dry mouth a lot	0	1	2	3
△	I couldn't seem to feel any positive feeling at all	0	1	2	3
□	I experienced breathing difficulty	0	1	2	3
△	I found it hard to get things done	0	1	2	3

○	I was over reacting	0	1	2	3
□	I was trembling (eg. In the hands)	0	1	2	3
○	I felt a lot of nervous energy	0	1	2	3
□	I was worried about situations in which I might panic	0	1	2	3
△	I felt that I had nothing to look forward to	0	1	2	3
○	I found myself getting agitated and annoyed	0	1	2	3
□	I found it difficult to relax	0	1	2	3
△	I felt upset, heavy and blue	0	1	2	3
○	I was intolerant of anything that kept me from getting on with what I was doing	0	1	2	3
□	I felt I was close to panic	0	1	2	3
△	I was unable to become excited about anything	0	1	2	3
△	I felt I wasn't worth much as a person	0	1	2	3
○	I felt that I was rather sensitive	0	1	2	3
□	I was noticing my heart beat a lot	0	1	2	3
□	I felt scared, or worried without any good reason	0	1	2	3
△	I felt that life was meaningless	0	1	2	3

Adapted from Loveibond, S.H. & Loveibond, P.F. (1995). Manual for the Depression Anxiety Stress Scales (Lovibond and Lovibond 335-343)

Instructions: Add total for each

△ Total = _____   X 2 = _____   Depression Score

□ Total = _____   X 2 = _____   Anxiety Score

○ Total = _____   X 2 = _____   Stress Score

Have a look at DASS21 scoring chart to see how mild/ severe your current emotional states are:

DASS21 SCORING			
Rating	Depression	Anxiety	Stress
Normal	0 to 9	0 to 7	0 to 14
Mild	10 to 13	8 to 9	15 to 18
Moderate	14 to 20	10 to 14	19 to 25
Severe	21 to 27	15 to 19	26 to 33
Extremely Severe	28+	20+	34+

Disclaimer: Provided to you by LLF for educational purposes only. If there is an indication you might be depressed, or a risk to yourself or others please seek help of a mental health professional professional or your medical doctor. Contact Get Real International for additional information, tools and support.

This book was written for *everyone*. There is not a single person who would not benefit from what is found here. However, this book has been especially written for those of you who want to make a change for the better. Maybe you feel a little different from everyone else, or you want to create a life that's special. As a result, you might be struggling to feel you are on the right track. You may even be suffering with things like depression, lack of focus, stress, anxiety, anger, or a feeling of being lost in the world.

You need only take a quick look at mental health and suicide statistics worldwide to see what is really happening. Young people (those aged ten – twenty-five) represent the majority of those people impacted by mental health struggles. The world is failing young people. Did you know that the number - one cause of death in young people is suicide?[1] Too many young people are battling with issues and addictions. Too many have a general lack of interest in the lives they are currently living. This is a tragedy that is inexcusable - and completely preventable.

This call for change has been heard! There are many things wrong with the way you have been shown how to handle life and your various feelings. All of this is about to change. The only thing you need to do is say "yes". It doesn't matter if it's a screaming "Hell yes!" or a tiny squeak. When you say "yes" everything begins to change.

So what do you say?

Life Hack #1: Learn to Ask for Help

Many people go all the way through life and never learn how to ask for help. It's such a simple thing, but sometimes we don't realise when help is needed. You don't have to know all the answers or where the support will come from. The very act of asking is the right place to start.

In this hack you will learn:

- To discover what you really want
- To ask for it and let go
- How to recognise and receive that support

There is magic in knowing what you need and putting that need out there. You need to be clear about what you want and not be afraid to ask. Even if you are afraid – don't let that fear stop you. Like Natasha you can experience better relationships when you have the courage to ask for what you need.

---

[1] ("Australian Bureau Of Statistics, Australian Government")

Natasha

I was in a mentoring session with a fifteen-year-old girl, let's call her Natasha. She told me her relationship with her mother had been a three-year power struggle, with no closeness and constant fighting.

As she talked about it, I could hear the sadness in her voice. I asked her, "If you could ask your mum for anything, what would you ask her for? What do you need from her now?"

Tears began to stream down her face, much to her surprise. She whispered, "I just want her trust. I just want to be able to talk to her about things."

She shared, she had been afraid to admit this to herself because it felt like she could never have that with her mum. She realised that as a defence, she pushed her mum away. In saving herself from that possible rejection, she was in fact, creating it.

When she saw what she wanted and what she had been afraid of, she was able to ask for what she wanted. She could then work on everything that was an obstacle to that. Learning to ask for help, Natasha could then be supported in developing a more open relationship with her mum.

So what do you need help with right now? What do you wish was different?

If you could change anything, what would it be?

What are you struggling with? Write a few things down that first come to mind.

Don't judge or filter your thoughts, just get them down on paper right now.

_____

_____

_____

_____

_____

_____

_____

_____

Well done! Asking for help is the first step to receiving it.

Sometimes it's hard to know what we need help with, if you had some trouble answering that question, join the club.

Or you may think that the answers are obvious: "I want a million dollars" Awesome! Now let me ask you what will that really give you? Is it the freedom or opportunities it would give you? Is it power? Is it the feeling that buying stuff gives you? What do you really want from life? As you explore the answers to those questions, you will discover the deeper request for help. It is lying just beneath the surface.

Another common desire is for a relationship. If you wrote, "I want a boyfriend or a girlfriend," what will being in a relationship really give you? You might discover what you are really looking for is a feeling of being wanted, or safe, or simply feeling good about yourself. These are all natural aspirations. They are all essential human needs. When you are able to identify what is below your surface desires, you can then fulfil these needs in alternative, and sometimes healthier, ways.

Economist Manfred Max-Neef classifies essential human needs into nine elements: subsistence, protection, affection, understanding, participation, leisure, creativity, identity, and freedom[2]. It is natural for your desires to feed these essential human needs.

By discovering what you really want, you can be very specific and clear in your direction. This will prevent you from spending your whole life pursuing experience after experience, but never quite fulfilling the need. By identifying the essential human needs that motivate your desires, the unhealthy choices become a lot less compelling.

Let's explore!

What do you want right now? What else do you need? If you could ask for anything, what would you ask for?

_____

_____

_____

_____

_____

_____

_____

_____

_____

[2] (Stack 973-975)

Now, explore your answers. What do you think that would really give you? What would that bring to your life? How would it make you feel about yourself?

_____

_____

_____

_____

_____

_____

How would it feel to be experiencing those things in your life right now? What would your life be like?

_____

_____

_____

_____

_____

_____

_____

As you discover the deeper request, life may bring this to you in unexpected ways. It may or may not be the boyfriend or girlfriend who makes you feel good about yourself. You may discover your self-esteem boost some other way. See what happens.

Way More Than a Bucket List

For real and lasting change in your life you must be willing to grow. Like everything in life, growth is subject to natural laws, seasons and patterns. To make these patterns work for you, it helps first to understand them.

There is a scientific principle known as Liebig's Law of the minimum[3]. While this process is used to analyse soil and plant growth, it can also be fully applied to your life. It teaches that growth is controlled not by circumstances and resources, but by what you may lack in your life or the limiting factors you may face.

When you are missing some essential key for your happiness, it's like having a leaking bucket and repairing it in the wrong place. The bucket will only ever be able to fill to the lowest broken point.

Working with thousands of people over the years, I have identified seven crucial areas for human growth and potential. I have observed that each of these areas need to be taken care of, to create that overall experience of wellbeing and fulfilment. If one area is lacking it will limit your overall potential. Once you know how to concentrate your efforts you know where to focus. Aimee's story will show you how this can apply to life.

---

[3] (Morgan and Watkinson 73-78)

Here's an example of how it looks:

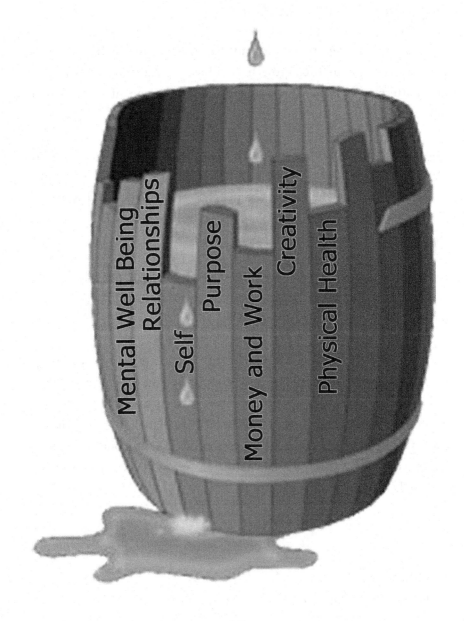

Aimee

Another girl I worked with, this time I will call Aimee, was a beautiful fifteen-year-old girl with everything going for her. She lived in a really nice home, was doing well at school, on an athletic scholarship, at one of the best schools in the city. She was great to talk to, had a close group of friends, took wonderful care of her health and was in fantastic shape.

Aimee also suffered with depression. When we worked together, I was able to see that her relationship with her family, her father, and even her boyfriend were all very disconnected. She was not able to communicate, or feel close to any of them.

No matter how much time, energy and care she put into every other aspect of her life, or her less important relationships with her friends, this part of her life constantly brought her down. Her disconnected close relationships, were the leak in her bucket. Recognising this made it so much easier to focus her attention on what needed to change. As we addressed this one piece at a time, her overall happiness and wellbeing skyrocketed. It had caught up to the rest of her already great life.

How about you do your own check up? Look at each area of your life. Celebrate what you are achieving. Identify what you would like to be different.

Activity:

Keeping the Leaky Bucket picture in front of you. Complete the following two lists for EACH area.

1. What are you happy with, proud of and enjoying in this area? Take time to celebrate. Think of things at home, at school, with friends and personally. What are you pleased with?

2. What do you wish was different? What do you want to change, grow or work on? Even if you don't know how, think about what is holding you back or annoying you.

When you are doing this sometimes goals pop up. Write them down if they do. We will come back to your goals later. There is no need to stress if your goals don't pop up now.

This will become your motivation for change, so be sure to find the most powerful motivators possible. Once you have finished the exercise look back over this table and *__highlight 1 or 2 areas__* to focus on as you work through the rest of the book. Working on these existing limiting factors will help you get the most out of your life. Change is then easier, because it starts with you, and therefore it's in your control.

AREA	WHAT I'M PLEASED WITH	WHAT I WISH WAS DIFFERENT	GOAL/ ACTION
SELF			
RELATIONSHIPS			
PHYSICAL HEALTH			
EMOTIONS/ MENTAL			
PURPOSE/ PASSION			
MONEY/WORK			
CREATIVITY			

The Game Changers

Ever wondered what really makes you feel so up and down emotionally? One day we can be on top of the world. The next day we can be deep at the bottom of the ocean. So how do you ride these emotional waves without going under?

Life Hack #2: There is Nothing "Wrong" with How You Feel

In this hack you will learn how to:

- Deal easily with all emotions – no judgement
- Catch your strategies you use to hide things and end up hurting you
- Change the things you want to

The real problem is that you have been lied to – we all have. All our lives we are taught that some feelings are good and some are bad. The bad ones must be fixed.

Think about the first response people offer when they see someone emotional. "What's wrong?" is the inevitable question. We keep reinforcing the belief that these 'bad emotions' are wrong. Then, we adopt various strategies in an attempt to avoid feeling that way. We distract ourselves in activity or numb out in front of a screen to avoid potential pain.

This is a natural learning process. When you put your hand on something hot and burn yourself, you don't keep touching it. The same response can automatically kick in when it comes to emotional pain. But, unfortunately it is a very different thing.

Emotional pain cannot resolve itself until you face it and acclimatise to it. When you avoid emotional pain it can make you feel very stuck. Sound familiar? What if there was nothing 'wrong' with your feelings – ever? No matter what you are feeling, what if you didn't fix it, try to change it, avoid it? What if you just let it be? How would that change things for you?

Growing up, I didn't have the tools I needed to deal with my past so it all got stored it in "my little box of stuff." My favoured strategy was to keep on the move. I travelled like a gypsy from town to town, country to country all in the name of adventure. When I couldn't physically be on the move, I would be running away into the refuge of my imagination.

This was my game, set up by my mind to help me avoid/fix some *big, bad feeling*. While I was literally running around the world away from the pain inside me, of course I was carrying it with me. That's the problem, these avoidance strategies never work. They often lead us right to the pain we are trying to avoid. It has been said, "on the path you take trying to avoid your destiny, you meet it." By avoiding facing my past, I possibly led myself to more of these painful experiences because I didn't stop to learn my lessons.

My gypsy game wasn't so easy to play when I married and had children of my own. I couldn't just up and go when things got tough. During a painful divorce, I was finally forced to face the emotional pain I had been running from over the years. It was like a door opened inside me and it all came rushing out.

I found the courage to meet all the fears and tears that had been stuffed somewhere inside me since I was a child. It was a special time in my life

15

when I allowed all of my feeling and just let them be. It was such a relief, like the weight of the world had been lifted off my shoulders. I was free.

Catching Your Games.

Your games are strategies that take attention away from how you are feeling. Be it angry, scared, jealous, or worried, we tend to avoid anything that feels uncomfortable. However, the feelings just sit there waiting for us the strategies aren't a solution at all. Eventually, the time must come to resolve them. If you know your avoidance strategies, you can act on this knowledge and take charge of your life. Here are some common games and strategies. See if you recognise any.

- **Blame/projection:**
  Rather than feeling the anger, people will often blame the person or object that has triggered the anger. So it's mum's fault you are angry because she said "no" to something. Or it's the computer's fault it won't save something. You can miss the opportunity to explore and release that anger in a healthy way when you make it 'their' fault and project the cause of the feeling onto someone or something else.

- **Shut down, or put it to sleep:**
  You can be overwhelmed by strong emotions like grief, anger, or terror. Instead of feeling the power of them you can unknowingly try to put the feeling to sleep by using all your energy to keep it under control.

  Some people do this by physically getting very tired and depressed. Other people use substances like drugs, alcohol or 'comfort eating' and even too much gaming. Minimizing things saying "it's ok", when it's really not, is another way of playing things down. These games leave you unable to feel what is really going on.

- **Cover it up, burying feelings:**
  For some, anger can be a cover for everything else. Feeling angry can be more acceptable than admitting to feeling down, weak, or hurt. So on the surface these emotions come out like anger. "Playing nice" is another way to play this game, by putting a smile over the top of just about anything to cover what you are truly feeling. Then it stays there brewing underneath the surface.

- **Run away:**
  Get busy physically or in the mind, or actually run away, like I did, moving from place to place. This can also look like high-pressured achievements one after another.

- **Dramatize or tell "poor me" stories:**
  Talk all about what has happened rather than how it makes you feel. Get stuck in the victim mentality, thinking it's not fair, your life is so hard, no one "get's you".

  Getting stuck in these stories you can become identified in them. This can lead to self-destructive or physically harming behaviors. When this occurs it is confirmation of how flawed you are and how hard you have it. Getting lost in these stories and what happened to you doesn't allow you to connect with the emotions and resolve them.

- **Hyping up your identity:**
  Who you think you are can be fragile. You may cover up feelings of low self-esteem or lack of confidence, by trying to fit in and belong. You can become so focused on what to wear, do and be that your identity becomes a pressure. When this happens you may assert, protect and maintain this hyped up sense of self so much you get lost in it.

- **Hide from the world**:
  When you retreat inside for safety and shut the rest of the world out, you can get lost. When you are disconnected from the outside world it can be an anxious, lonely and terrifying place to live. You become lost in distractions with gaming, or devices. While this might appear like it's meeting your human need for connection, it is doing the opposite. This can spiral like an addiction and spin into feelings of depression and anxiety.

- **Bully, boss or try to take control**:
  To feel powerful, strong and safe, to avoid feelings of things being out of control you can be controlling and forceful. Avoiding softer feelings you can miss some of the best parts of being alive. You miss so much joy and love getting stuck in the habit of controlling everything and everyone.

- **Trying to be perfect**:
  To avoid potential conflict or the feeling of disapproval you can get totally stuck in a people pleasing habit. Trying to be more perfect, to desperately meet unrealistic expectations. Life becomes very intense, high pressured, and unsustainable. It's an impossible task as we are all beautifully imperfect at the core, so this has you running from a constant wave of failure.

People use these games and many more. No two games are exactly the same. As individuals, people play out these games differently. So to really know yourself, you must know your game. Then you can choose to play the game of life – or keep letting it play you.

Let's explore:

Which of these games have you played? Write them down?

_____

_____

_____

How do you play them? What else have you done to avoid feeling 'bad' or uncomfortable feelings?

_____

_____

_____

What else? (keep going and get down as many or few as you like)

_____

_____

_____

What games/strategies do you use with your friends or your family?

_____

_____

_____

What has this cost you? How has this limited you?

_____

_____

_____

How has this affected you and your life?

_____

_____

_____

What does it feel like to be stuck in these games?

_____

_____

_____

What does that mean for your life?

_____

_____

_____

How does this really make you feel? (Allow yourself to just feel that… let it be – be honest with yourself)

_____

_____

_____

Now that you have explored your games… want to try something different?

What if you did something radical – and stopped avoiding your feelings and started feeling? Once you learn to master your feelings, rather than just acting them out, you have your power back. Angie's story helps you see a bit clearer how these games work.

Angie

Angie, a 15- year-old girl I have been coaching, when we first started working together she was so stuck in fear and anxiety. She found it hard to leave the house. She had trouble getting to school and staying for more than a few hours. The fear was so strong it would make her physically sick. She hated it and she wanted change, but the fear had got so stuck in her body that she didn't know how to resolve it.

She was avoiding the feeling of fear by dedicating all her hours to her Facebook page and games. She was stuck in her stories justifying why she was living this way.

After a year of being stuck at home, the fear tracked her down. Her strategy was no longer working. Her isolated life was making the fear and anxiety much worse. She had become trapped in her own game and hated being stuck at home.

By scribbling the feelings all out on a big piece of paper, she finally stopped running from the fear, trying to control it and wishing it would go away. She learned to feel all of it. She cried, shook and panicked. But she kept drawing it all out. Thinking of everything that ever made her feel afraid, it got intense for a few seconds. Then it popped. She felt herself falling into a big black pit. Tears kept falling down her face as she kept scribbling. The colours changed from dark to light. She began laughing. Through the laughter and the tears she said, "there is nothing here to be afraid of. I've been afraid of nothing." She felt this huge wave of relief. Then she felt so much joy. I gave her a fresh bit of paper and asked her to paint that joy. She did this with a huge smile on her face. From this moment on she had a way to conquer her fear every time it rose up and keep moving forward with her life.

Within days Angie was back at school. She told me after a few weeks she didn't feel afraid anymore. She explained, it was like she wore out all the fear and it was replaced with feeling joy. In time, the fear and anxiety disappeared all together and she was free.

This is what is possible for everyone. If you have the courage to face what you have been avoiding.

So many personal problems and difficulties dealing with the world around us are caused by people trying to control or change how they are feeling. However, you can acknowledge at any moment that feelings are an impermanent passing state. If you let them pass, by simply allowing them, the next feeling will come.

You don't have to like how you feel all the time. Have a look around you. Life is full of contrasting colours. You need to experience all of them to appreciate life fully.

Like Angie, treating emotions this way will totally shift your relationship with all feelings. You will become less dragged around by your feelings and more in control of your life. Most adults around you haven't mastered this yet. You will be well ahead of the game.

Give it a try – feel it

Step 1: Stop avoiding

Now having spotted a few of your emotional avoidance games, it's time to STOP. What would you have to feel if you couldn't cover it up that way? Find just one feeling that you might have been avoiding through your life. For Angie it was fear. What is it for you? You can even think of a feeling you have experienced recently, or now.

Step 2: Where is it

Whatever it is, even if it's really small - feel it, observe it in your body. For some people it can even feel like physical pain or a sick feeling. Focus all of your attention on it. Is it in your heart, or your tummy or your fists? It might make you feel wired, anxious, hot, sick. Let it happen. Let your muscles around it relax, like inside you are saying "yes" to it. Gently, start to open the lid on that box. Let the feelings just flow, until the emotion starts to grow or come to the surface more. Allow it to be felt. Quietly, feel the sensation of it in your body.

In a few seconds it changes, opens out, pops and gets lighter. Let it flow through your body. You don't need to hype it up, make pictures or stories about it. Feel yourself relax and soften the muscles in your body.

Step 3: Acclimatize and let it change

Go right into the feeling, rather than tensing up or avoiding it. Keep going, even if it gets boring, or really intense. Notice if your games pop up and don't play them. Keep your attention on the feelings, relaxing into it more and more.

Soon another feeling will come. They only take a few seconds each. They can't last longer than fourteen seconds, if you just feel it. Don't add a story to it or distract yourself. If you feel stuck remember stuck is just a feeling, so do the same with that feeling. Let it take its time. You will usually feel two or three different types of heavy, darker, hotter feelings. Then it opens out into something lighter, more spacious.

This is what happens when you acclimatize to a feeling. It's similar to your body's response to hot weather when the seasons change. At the beginning of summer, it feels crazy hot. Then your body gets more and more used to the heat, and then it changes again.

Step 4: Stay here and take action:

In just a few minutes being with your emotions in this way you will start feeling clearer, happier and eventually a lighter feeling takes over. You can then take action from that clearer space, where you are not running from something inside.

Experiment with it – it's really safe just to allow feelings, and see what happens for you.

Adapted processes[4]

What feeling did you find?

_____

What did it change to?

_____

How do you feel now?

_____

_____

[4] (Bays)

EMOTIONAL PAIN CAN'T BE KICKED UNTIL YOU FACE IT

FOR THAT YOU MUST STOP AVOIDING IT!

Tamsyn Rosenberg
Keepin it real!

Break Up With Your Past

Life slings at you a series of experiences and challenges to test your resolve as well as to help you learn. Sometimes, it can feel like the sun will never quite shine the same and that your life is forever changed. These experiences sometimes raise unresolvable issues.

Really all this means is that you have met a "game changer." Welcome to the big league. Here's the secret – life will now give you everything you need to make it through. So get ready, be greedy, milk it for every lesson you can get. Once you have really received what it's trying to teach you it finishes. Sometimes that takes years and sometimes it only takes a few moments. It is not in your control how it unfolds. You didn't ask for this, but you can choose to surrender to it.

Save your energy for taking all you need to learn and transform into the person you are now becoming. Then what you will notice, out the other side is a new version of you emerging, stronger, more courageous, wise and with a new found gift of perspective. This game changer won't kill you, but it really will transform you – if you allow it to.

My big game changer began when I was four-years-old, and I have let this experience be one of my biggest life lessons.

I have always considered myself a Daddy's girl. I waited for that moment each day for Dad to come home from work. I would sit on his lap and listen to his deep voice echoing in his chest. Those precious moments got fewer as I grew. The fighting got more frequent and loud between my parents. My place on Dad's lap at the end of the day slowly turned into being sent to my room early, or feeling like I was in the way. My sister and I would cuddle and chat in our room listening to the roar of fighting through the floorboards. Then came the quiet. The quiet of Dad not coming home for dinner. The quiet sadness and the whispering in the house.

One Christmas Eve there was a fight like no other. We were grabbed from our rooms and put in the car. I watched our family home get smaller and smaller as we drove away without dad. There was so much pain, mine and my family's. I could feel it all and I felt so lost. I desperately wanted to go home, and I couldn't stop my tears. I tried to make my sadness quiet. It took nearly all of my energy to get those tears to stop.

We arrived at a skinny little mid-terraced house and it was dark. We were told this would be our new home, new life and new Dad. I looked down as I stepped inside the front doorway. I imagined that this doorway was magic as I stepped through. I imagined I was stepping into a new land, where I would forget all pain and I would start again.

I learned to love my new dad. But, I never stopped looking out of the window for my old Dad to visit. Whenever we were not together I missed him so much. It was a hole in me that I couldn't fill.

My family kept changing over the years, as families do. My baby sister was born. My new Dad didn't play with me as much. He loved having a baby. They were so happy together and I felt lost. Every change left me feeling that lost feeling hiding inside of me. I didn't know where home was anymore.

One Saturday morning, visiting my old Dad, we went to the beach. I listened to his familiar deep voice echoing in his chest as we walked and talked. I felt that safe feeling. I was relaxing in that feeling when his words caught my attention. "You are moving to Australia, we won't be able to see each other when you move. I'm sorry."

Something started spinning and an aching pain landed in my chest. I froze and my dad kept walking down the beach. I stood there totally alone feeling so little and the world seemed so huge.

Then I heard a small voice inside all my sadness. She was saying, *"it's ok, now you only have yourself. You can't depend on anyone. You have to do it all yourself. You are going to be ok. You can do it all yourself."*

I swallowed my tears. I didn't ask him to fight for me or if I could stay. I gave up and learned very young to rely on myself. I decided from now on I would learn to take care of myself. I didn't notice the hard shell that appeared around my heart.

Losing my Dad, my family, my home and then my country was my first Game Changer. I just couldn't handle it all at the time. So I packed that sadness into "my little box of stuff."

We moved to Australia. In the years that followed, I began the clever game of running from pain; town-to-town, school-to-school, country-to-country, back and forward from Australia to England. Before I turned twenty-two, I travelled around the world three times. Without realising I was searching everywhere for that safe place, that home, I lost in my childhood. I met amazing teachers completing my studies and working hard to save for the next big adventure. I only realise now how much I was running away and what I was desperately searching for.

In time, I stopped looking for safety and the feeling of belonging in different places. I started to search for answers to that mysterious question; "who am I?" I made a study of my family history, learning about my roots and heritage. I found great peace in my prayers and in the study of human behaviour. Who I am and how to heal from past started to reveal itself to me a little piece at a time.

Life Hack #3: How to Finish with the "Game Changers"

In this hack you will learn how to:

- Learn from the past and move on
- Be stronger for what has happened to you rather than held back by it
- Heal no matter what

Accept this will take whatever time it needs, surrender to the process and don't try to rush it. Remember that it all becomes lighter and lighter in time. The joyful times will get more common and the sadder times will get further apart, until they just gently disappear. This will pass, eventually, everything always does. When you are ready, these steps will walk you through this experience so you come out on top:

1. Trust life and yourself that this is happening so the best version of you can emerge from the ashes of this experience. You may not see the whole picture along the way, so simply trust. Be willing to step out into the dark and know that life has got you.

2. Be willing to say "yes" to it – open your hands on the experience and let it be your teacher. This is possible, no matter how dark, devastating and twisted the experience is.

3. Feel everything you are feeling, all the way to the end. Sit in the river of feelings and let them all come and all go.

4. Take every opportunity to be honest and open around your feelings. Talk to the people involved in person if you can. Otherwise in your imagination will do and say everything. To your brain it's the same process, real or imagined. You can resolve it if you just speak all your words out loud.

5. When you are ready - forgive. You are doing this for you, not them. This allows you to take that big rock out of your emotional

backpack you have been carrying around and put it down. Once that decision to forgive has been made, all the pain, resentment, hurt and grief will go over time. Forgiveness doesn't make the action or behaviour ok. It doesn't mean you even want the person in your life again. You might, but it doesn't mean that. It means that you understand they were doing the best they could at the time. Accepting this is forgiving them and letting it go.

So ask yourself, can you forgive them? Can you really let go? If you can't yet, it simply means you have more words to speak, more to share. When it's all been said forgiveness will be the natural side effect. So cry your tears, feel the rage, hate the hate and then when it's all said and done... forgive.

6.   Watch your thoughts and choose which ones to follow. Notice if you keep adding painful thoughts, pictures and stories to it like: "this means I'll never be good enough to;" or "I'll never feel any better, this is never going to end, I can't get through this." This self-talk adds fuel to a fire that is trying to burn itself out. This will keep you stuck, rather than allowing you to keep moving through it. It will eat into your overall happiness. These kinds of thoughts will keep having a damaging effect you even when you are feeling. This is because you will still be nursing the bruises of your own internal beating and harmful beliefs. If you catch yourself getting dark in your thoughts, simply say "stop." Put an end to them.

7.   Learn the life lesson. As you rise from the ashes share only the lesson. Let the experience truly finish. Don't keep resurrecting it by dramatising the story of it over and over or taking up some victim role. Share your incredible lessons. Let these grow and deepen by allowing others to learn from what you have discovered. This is what it is to evolve.

8. Let these lessons finish the games and strategies you have played in the past. You have evolved. Now get to know yourself again.

9. It's ok to move on. Give yourself permission to laugh and play. Know you have your whole life ahead of you and you will fill it with so much beauty and magic. This is a time of healing so let it happen. When it's complete, get stuck into the magic of the next stage of life waiting for you.

Whether you know it or not you are unlimited. You are all potential.

Life is and will continue to help you discover this again and again. That's the deal. Life will only give you what you can handle. So if it all feels tough right now, know you are too.

Life will take your relationships that you cling to. It will take who you think you are and mix it all up, stripping you bare at times. These are very special times. These "game changers" are what finish the games we play. At these times, with nothing but the ashes, you glimpse your infinite potential. You will rise from these experiences transformed by all you discover. So when this visitor arrives at your door, greet it on your knees and be grateful as you allow your greatest teacher in. Let the game changer – be the game finisher you have asked for.

YOU HAVE AMAZING POTENTIAL WITHIN YOU, DISCOVER HOW STRONG YOU ARE

IF LIFE IS TOUGH RIGHT NOW IT'S COS YOU ARE TOO!!

Tamsyn Rosenberg
Keepin it real!

Get It Off Your Chest

Unspoken words can have you feeling misunderstood and disconnected from those around you. Do you hold back things you need to talk about? This doesn't mean just saying what you think others want to hear. No matter what you share with exposure the connection with that person becomes stronger. However, when you hold words back, or sugar coat things, resentment and disconnection builds. If you keep things to yourself, you will feel more alone and like nobody understands you. But it's really you not letting them in.

Imagine your body is like a jar full of rocks. Each of these rocks are unspoken words that must be said. Your body is made up of billions of cells and each of these cells store memories and unresolved pain from everything that happens to you in life. To move past these experiences you must get those words out of your cells and off your chest. Only then will you be able to enjoy closer more connected relationships.

With many families I work with, disconnection has become the 'norm'. It's not working. No one knows what needs to change because there is little to no communication. This was certainly the case for Felicity and her family.

Felicity

When I first walked into Felicity's home it felt cold and lonely. There were four people living there and nobody had anything to say to each other. Each person appeared to have their own designated corner of the house and the "do not disturb" signs were up.

When I spoke to Felicity about what she was going through she was lost in the blame game. According to Felicity, her parents sucked, nobody understood her and her life was really hard. Her strategy was to play the victim and get lost in her own stories. Anxiety and depression followed as a natural consequence of consistently feeling so disconnected and alone.

This family could have continued along this path. Felicity had started to rely more on her group of friends than her parents for guidance. This led her to experiment with drugs, guys and life choices without considering the potential consequences. To change the direction the whole family needed to try something radical – the truth. Real, raw honesty was needed.

They began making some difficult changes. Rather than shutting down, keeping things to themselves, they were asked to play some communication games. The first few times it was messy. It came out heated, blaming each other, feelings got hurt and words got twisted. But in the process they each began listening again. I guided them to clarify things and to practice listening from the other person's perspective. Put themselves in each other's shoes. They practiced understanding each other, rather than fixing things or blaming each other.

It didn't change things over night. But a little bit at a time truth did it's work. Being more open and honest about their experiences allowed them to feel more connected and understood over time. The atmosphere changed. The air grew warmer somehow.

On my last visit with the family, the parents unexpectedly opened up. They shared with me that these exercises had not only saved their connection with their daughter, but their marriage as well. Unbeknown to me, they had also been experiencing marriage difficulties and were wondering if their relationship would survive. They were so amazed at the turn around in their home by allowing the truth to be spoken in this way. Felicity was happier and the anxiety she had been struggling with was resolved. They were able to make this their new "norm."

In my experience this is the ultimate relationship saver. When you communicate honestly with another person, it's a deep healing. It's not about right and wrong. Truth is different for everyone. We each have a different picture or perception.

As you each share from your own view, different filters will determine each picture. Both your pictures are essentially right. So this sharing is about getting it all out, not about winning an argument. This really changes how you relate with everyone you care about.

In this diagram[5] it illustrates what impacts your perspective on any external event:

---

[5] ("Perception Is Not Reality |")

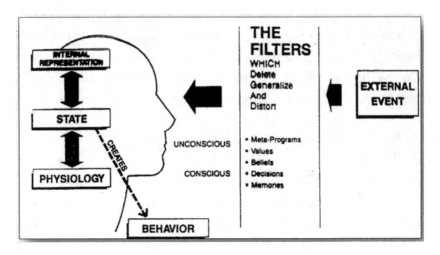

For example, if Felicity stuck to her story that her parents just didn't get her, she would never have opened up and given the game a chance to work. This would have meant her viewing any discussion with her parents as them being uncaring and disconnected from her reality. This would have been another affirmation to why her life was so hard. This perspective would distort what she was experiencing outside and then alter her internal state, leaving her anxious and depressed. This would then affect her ongoing behaviour. Do you see how the cycle of perception can continue to effect someone's perception?

Felicity was brave enough to explore her parents' perspective as well as share her own. This meant light could be shed on the whole picture. Her understanding the situation from all sides allowed her to alter her beliefs. This changed her internal emotional state. Everyone experiences their own picture and has their own reaction. For us to heal we need to have a glimpse into someone else's picture.

I learned the lesson of how different perception creates different pictures, when I wanted to return to England to meet my dad at sixteen-years-old. I hadn't seen him since we moved to Australia after my parent's divorce. It had been 12 years. I wanted to follow my heart, meet my Dad and ask some of the questions that I had been wrestling with for years.

I was travelling alone. On the final decent into London after the pilot announced we would soon be landing, a wall of panic hit me. There was an old lady sitting next to me.

She said gently, "my dear you have gone as white as a ghost. It's ok, flying is very safe."

I crumbled in her kindness and the tears escaped my eyes. I explained I wasn't afraid of flying. But I was terrified to meet this stranger that was my Dad. All my fears found me in that second. "Was I enough? Would he love me? Why didn't he want me? Why didn't he fight for me? Why didn't he stay in touch? What was wrong with me?"

This angel in the sky gently held my hand as I cried. She said, "if he doesn't love you he's crazy. You are going to be fine. You are very brave." She held my hand till we landed. Then she was gone.

I stood alone before a crowd of faces and I froze. Just like that little girl on the beach all those years ago. I felt so little and lost. I realised in that moment I didn't even know what he looked like. I felt so frightened scanning the sea of strangers. Then the sound of that deep voice broke my thoughts and grabbed me from my spiralling fear. "Twelve years is a long time my girl." He hugged me. I didn't recognise his face. In the months that followed I got to know him, a little bit at a time.

We tried to fill in the spaces of the "dark days" as he called them. We shared stories. He talked about his version of what happened in my parent's marriage. Their stories were so different. I struggled to figure out which story was right. At some point I got it; there was no wrong or right. I gave up needing to understand anything about the past. These stories had nothing to do with me. Giving up the need to understand was the most peaceful feeling I have known.

I learnt that everyone has a different perception about the events in their lives. I discovered there are as many versions of truth as there are people.

The best we can do is listen to each other with compassion and learn to forgive human error. So this is what I did - I stopped asking why. I just became curious about who my father was and what he has been through. Years before, I heard my mother's experience and had learnt all she had to teach me. Something shifted in me through this process. The world began to feel like home and people I loved felt like family. I was able to let go of the past, or rather the grasp it had on me. I could really move on. Of course it didn't change what happened. But it did change my perception. The result for me was peace.

Life Hack #4: Better Out Than In

In this hack you will learn how to:

- Get everything off your chest without ever offending anyone
- Move past resentment and anger
- Communicate everything clearly and feel amazing in the process

Are you ready to learn to listen deeply, to be curious about someone else's picture? To do this, you have to step into their shoes. You need to attempt to really understand, without making any of it about you. It takes a certain level of compassion to understand another person's view. The best thing about this game is that you don't need to agree on anything to resolve a situation, then forgive and move on.

Activity: "Better out than in" communication game

To play this game you can play it with the person you are feeling disconnected from and really have this conversation with them. Or if they are not ready for that, or it's not possible you can imagine they are listening. It works just the same. You don't have to wait for them for you to find peace or a resolution.

1. Imagine the other person, or ask someone to role-play them for you. The other person will listen only. For this to be effective,

only one person talks at a time. For example, if it's your Mum you feel disconnected from, imagine her listening. If you feel too silly talking out loud, you can write this as a letter. However, it's much better to look a little crazy and speak out loud as if you are talking directly to them.

2. Give yourself permission to speak all the things that you have never said, or that you think you "shouldn't" or "couldn't" say at the time. Speak out loud as if speaking right to them. Tell them everything about how it makes you feel. Expose all of your feelings. Be prepared to be a little vulnerable. The secret with this is to share how you feel, rather than the story or fact telling. Really speak from the emotion in it all. How did it make you feel? Share that with them. What couldn't you say before, or have you been holding back? Get it all out.

3. If someone is helping you with this activity, or you are speaking in real life with the person, it's their job to listen. Every now and then they can say "thanks" and encourage you to keep sharing. They don't respond and talk about things at this stage, or share their perspective. This exercise is about getting everything off your chest and them listening to your perspective. They might keep you talking by asking, "what else have you got to say? Or encouraging you, saying, "thanks… keep going… thanks, and…. What else…" Keep talking and sharing you're your feelings until you feel you have reached the bottom of the barrel. Remember the aim is to get all those stored "rocks" out of your cells.

4. Ask yourself if you have got it all off your chest and felt it all. Even if their behaviour/actions weren't ok, are you able to forgive the person? (If you don't feel ready to forgive the person – keep talking to them until you can)

Take five minute turns each. Swap roles until you have everything off your chest from each perspective. One person speaks while the other person simply listens. This isn't about having the same opinion, or taking anything personally. This game means that it doesn't matter who is right and wrong. Keep going back and forward in turns, until there is nothing left to say, then forgiveness is simple. The air will feel lighter when everything is done. Everyone gets it all off their chest and it's better out than in!

Remarkably, no matter what had to be said, you will feel lighter. No matter how hard it is to hear it, it's better out than in. Then forgiveness should just be natural. Let yourself forgive. There is nothing left for you to hang on to. If you don't feel able to, just keep talking.

This can be played as a game, or it may be a style of communication you choose to use in relating with others. When all is said and done you will be able to forgive for yourself, and you are free.

Be the Real Thing

Life Hack #5: There are No Mistakes, Only Learning:

In this hack you will learn:

- How to give yourself permission to live and learn
- To be yourself and give up all the pretending
- Be more comfortable in yourself

Right through life everyone is learning through trial and error. Adults might look like they have got it all sorted, but everyone is stumbling their way through making their fair share of mistakes. It's part of life. There really is no such thing as mistakes. There is only learning. The most important thing you can make a study of is you. Your life experiences and your patterns have so much to teach you. It's such an empowering thing to do, because once you have seen your patterns, you can change them.

During my professional training, I was asked to start observing my behaviour patterns. It was then I discovered that one of these patterns was shaping my whole personality.

I had learned from a young age how to hide what I was really feeling. My memories of leaving England when I was four-years-old are very hazy. But I do remember clearly the sadness in leaving my Gran, my family and what I'd known as home. I swallowed the pain and tried to pretend I was not bothered by the changes. I wanted to be a good girl. There were also aspects of the change that felt like an adventure so I tried to focus on those.

In an attempt to show I was brave and could take care of myself, I tried to hide the natural grief and confusion that came with such a big move. At night I would open the doors on my tears, letting them flow. In the morning, I would lock them back up, put a smile on my face, put my "costume" on to go out into the world. My new Dad had joined the air force. This meant a lot of moving. My sister and I once counted twenty schools we attended. I could make friends and lose them without crying. I got good at putting on the masks of what I thought people wanted me to be, rather than being myself. This way I could slot quickly in any group so I wasn't alone. I wanted to fit in and find my place in the world. learned to create layers of myself and show different things to different people. But the truth was always hurting inside. The truth was I never felt like I belonged.

I would pray a lot and imagined God was like a dad looking over me. Especially when the fighting would happen. I grew up in a big family, it could get loud. With each new child came more stress. The stress sometimes triggered more fighting. Every now and then someone would walk out with a bag, overwhelmed and frustrated. We would cry thinking they had gone forever. When they returned it was all forgotten until next time.

One year the fighting about my big sister got increasingly bad. Something changed at home. Decisions were made behind closed doors. My big sister, my best friend, was gone. She had been sent back to England to live with our Dad. This time I couldn't swallow the tears. I hated my family and I couldn't stop the hate. I couldn't understand or change any of it. The fate of everyone I loved was out of my control. Something was breaking and I needed to stop it. We had always had each other. Losing her was too much to bear.

Then I heard that voice, *"Tam… it's ok… now you just have you. You can't depend on any Dad, on family, on things or home. Now you have to do it all yourself. You are going to be ok. You can do it all yourself."*

I got up from my sadness and my pain. I dusted myself off. I pulled away from my family just a little bit more. I decided it was my job to be the grown up. I put my childhood in a box with all my tears. I locked it up. No one ever knew I was struggling behind that brave face, my well-constructed mask. Just because I was saying it was ok, didn't mean it was.

I had forgotten how to show what was I was really feeling. I learned to be "the good girl," be the responsible one and keep it all together for everyone else. Over years of not allowing myself to be real I got more depressed, anxious and felt alone in everything. The biggest cost of this game was that I stopped letting people in. I started to see even my friends and family from behind the walls I built. They would never have known. I always smiled and looked happy on the outside. Only I knew the pattern I was stuck in.

Privately, I struggled with anxiety and depression. I learned to "do nice" and put a smile over everything. These patterns remained stuck until much later in life, invisible even to me. Once I saw them, I was able to really change. I was able to clear the pain I had been avoiding. Slowly and carefully, my walls came down. I let people in to share my life. I learned how to build connection with others and thrive in that closeness. This was the key to the feelings of depression and anxiety resolving. They just let me go once I stopped pretending. Once I learned to be the real thing.

You don't have to wait until you are older to discover this freedom. Once you give yourself permission to be real with yourself and others you can unlock a deep self-acceptance and peace right now.

Let's have a go. Explore these questions and see what you discover about the *real* you.

ACTIVITY: Tell the truth to yourself and discover what is going on inside.

In what ways are you pretending your way through life, or hiding behind walls?

_____

_____

_____

_____

What other ways are you not just being totally yourself? Or do you feel you have to be a certain way with people?

_____

_____

_____

When I reflected on these things myself, I realised I was almost a different person for everyone, or for different groups of people I hang out with. How do you play? What are you never allowed to act like or be like around your friends, or around your family?

_____

_____

_____

_____

_____

_____

_____

_____

What masks or pretending do you think you put on around others?

_____

_____

_____

_____

_____

What would it feel like if you didn't do that, if you couldn't do that?

_____

_____

_____

_____

How would that make you feel? (Just allow that feeling until it moves through)

_____

_____

_____

_____

What do you think might happen if you were just completely yourself in every setting?

_____

_____

_____

What are you afraid would happen?

_____

How does that make you feel? (Just allow that feeling until it moves through)

What do think stands in the way of you being totally you… all the time?

_____

_____

_____

_____

_____

_____

Can you see that there are some ways, or many ways that you pretend or hide? It's easy to lose yourself in these masks and start to lose touch with who you are. I've found that by doing this, all I really achieve is the feeling of not being good enough. This is a lonely place to be.

In contrast when you stop all of the trying, you find a natural ease and peace.

Give it a try:

Activity: Close your eyes, and relax your breathing.

Imagine all those obstacles being gone. Imagine burning all those masks and patterns on a campfire, or throwing them into the sea, or disappearing, whereby you are free to be yourself, *really yourself,* all the time.

What does that feel like? In all the different parts of your life - at school, at home with your family, with your friends, your boyfriend or girlfriend, with people you don't know... on your own... what does it feel like to be totally you? Really feel this. If a scared or exposed feeling comes up, just feel it until it moves through. Keep lowering the walls and masks. Drop all the hard work and trying.

Just be... What does this really feel like? Imagine living your whole life like this. Imagine yourself as a child. What if you were always living like this? See the little version of you living this way. What does he/she look like? How do things seem different?

Imagine yourself growing up right through your life, simply being how you are. No pretending. Through your teen life, how does it change things? What about as an adult, in your career, with your friends, in your relationships? How does it feel to do life as your natural self?

If you like... you can commit to your life being this way, it's so easy, you can just *be.*

Opening your eyes… write about what your experienced:

_____

_____

_____

_____

This is the real thing – this is who you are.

I Know Who You Are - Do You?

Life Hack #6: Know and Be Yourself

In this hack you will learn all about:

- The different personality types and how that affects you
- Understanding others deeper than you ever have before
- Getting your power back by taking charge of your own personality games

How your personality develops throughout your life is so fascinating. It's actually a game you have learned to play really well, and it's possible to master your personality game.

There are nine different personality types. Everyone chooses an individual combination of the qualities of all the different personality types. These qualities make you behave, relate and think the way you do. When you act this way over and over, these choices shape your personality. Most of this you do without being aware. This is a natural part of your development; like breathing, you are not constantly thinking to breathe in and out. The exciting part is that it's always changing. You can choose the qualities of your personality to keep and the ones to discard. To discover your own patterns you need to understand the different personality types and their characteristics.

While you read about each different type, ask yourself "how do I do this?" or notice the patterns that sound familiar.

Type 1. The perfectionist: Needs to be perfect. They put a lot of pressure on themselves and others to get everything right. This personality type can be quite uptight and get outraged when they experience an injustice. They also get frustrated when they discover imperfection in others. They often think their way is the only way. They can be very judgmental. The core feeling they avoid is resentment and anger, which they turn inwards.

Type 2. The giver: Caring, warm and generous, often not able to stop himself or herself in the act of giving or serving. This activity of serving others is their way of trying to get love, attention and to feel needed. They are very focused on their appearance, being careful to feel loved and loveable. Secretly, they feel worthless and are trying to fill up that space by getting love externally. This personality type consistently avoids their own needs and the feeling of worthlessness.

Type 3. The achiever: Very driven and focused on their achievements and image. They identify themselves by the way they appear to others. Largly invested in labels, appearance or marks of success. Where success is not possible they will sometimes create an illusion of success by lying, name-dropping or exaggeration. They seek approval and attention from others constantly proving their worth. This strategy is used in an attempt to make them feel valued. Their core avoidance is failure.

Type 4. The creative: They often appear with a lot of flair and work to appear 'unique'. They can be very dramatic and make a big deal out of everything for attention. This personality type can be quite fun, artistic and emotionally up and down. They are usually hiding how broken, flawed and incomplete they feel inside. Attention for their uniqueness or their drama provides them some identity they can hide behind. They avoid feeling lost and empty.

Type 5. The thinker: They are all about their knowledge. They use their mind as a weapon, a source of feeling safe, prepared or superior. They are quiet and introverted. Often lost in thought, ideas, or their imagination. They can live isolated lives. Feelings of insecurity and fear are common. They are often struggling with overwhelming emotions they can't quite resolve. They avoid the unknown. They look to fill this up with more and more knowledge.

Type 6. The loyalist: The most loyal and efficient types are hard working and good at everything they apply themselves to. Their need to belong and fit in is important and creates a sense of security. Strong family and community members, they always seeking to fill their need to feel safe, secure, or part of something. They fear nearly everything, appearing very cautious and "doomsday" in their thinking. They try to avoid this fear by becoming competent at what they do and securing a safe place in the world. Their core avoidance is fear, and insecurity.

Type 7. The entertainer: Fun and outgoing they seek experience after experience to keep things light and exciting. They are often running from some kind of pain. They use the adrenalin of gathering experiences or the 'next thing' to keep them on the run from anything ordinary or heavy. They often find it hard to be sensitive to others because they can become quite manic and on the move. Their core avoidance is pain, or anything that looks like it might lead to pain.

Type 8. The leader: They need to be in control and in charge. They are trying to keep everyone safe and take responsibility for all those they consider family. They are usually the bullies and bosses of the world, commonly strong in their bodies and personalities. Their ability to love is just as strong. Often they feel like hurt kids deep inside. However, they rarely admit it, even to themselves. They can become weighed down in responsibility. They find it hard to feel love or ask for help. They are concerned this may look like weakness, or make them feel vulnerable.

Their core avoidance is weakness or anything that can be perceived as weakness.

Type 9. The peacemaker: This type wants to avoid conflict, keep the peace and keep everything under control. It's hard for them to say no or stand their ground as they don't want to cause conflict. They find it hard to clearly feel emotions and try to keep them supressed. They appear very laid back and relaxed. Their core avoidance is conflict and at a deeper level rage, so anything that might lead to that is also avoided.

As you read each of these, it's ok if you recognised a bit of yourself in them all. You actually do some of every personality type in different situations. However, one or two personality types you will be more like than the others.

To illustrate, imagine a situation where someone is being bullied at school. Let's look at how each personality type might respond to being bullied:

Type #1 Would lecture the bully with outrage at the injustice of their behaviour.

Type #2 Would Flatter them or see if there is anything they can do for them, to make the bully like them.

Type #3 Would try and talk their way out of it. They would drop a few names and spin a few stories about the black belt training they had in various martial arts (none of which are probably true).

Type #4 Would let it happen and cry victim. They would dramatise the events for attention, probably right into their adult life.

Type #5 Would act silly like a crazy clown and try to distract the bully with their behaviour while making a quick escape. Or they would try to throw facts at the bully and try to win with some kind of battle of the minds.

Type #6 Would get on side with the bully. They would see if they could join the group and probably do the bully's homework in the mean time.

Type #7 Would play some crazy music, dance about and give the bully such a fun time that they forget why they were there in the first place – The bully and the victim will probably end up best friends.

Type #8 Would very rarely be in this situation. They are usually the one doing the bullying. But when challenged they would beat the bully into submission and become the new leader and show everyone who's boss.

Type #9 Would try to talk their way out of the situation, either by making friends or taking the blame. They would do anything to avoid the fight. Or they would play down the situation, claiming it didn't bother them, until they forget about it.

Can you see the way different personality types will respond to the same situation in completely different ways, and with different agendas? You don't need to know what type you are. It is enough to recognise that there are different personality types, or Ego Types[6], at play. These different personality types inspire different strategies and behaviours when facing life's challenges and choices.

Let's Explore:

When you notice yourself in any of the personality games. Notice how you are playing it and what happens when you stop.

Ask yourself: "If I couldn't do this (this drama, or this taking charge, or trying desperately to fit in, or whatever else you notice) what would

---

[6] (Jaxon-Bear)

I have to feel?" The trick is to notice the feeling you are avoiding by playing that game.

_____

_____

Activity: Close your eyes, and relax your breathing. Feel what you would feel if you couldn't just play your normal personality game. If this game was not available to you, what would it feel like without it? (Feel that until it moves all the way through, and you feel free in some way.)

_____

_____

Now imagine letting go of all those games and personality patterns you don't want. Imagine burning them on a campfire, or throwing them away. You are free live your life with or without these patterns... any time you like. Now it is your choice. Take 3 deep breaths, and open your eyes when you are ready. Well done! This is what freedom of choice is all about.

Peter

When Peter, a 15 year-old client of mine, had a look at the patterns of the number 8 personality type he recognised so many of these games in himself. He could see the game was so out of control he had become aggressive and violent with his family. Ironically they were the very people he most wanted to love and protect. He spoke with me, about a time when his sister was younger and he had such a love for her, and would do anything to protect her. His version of that role had distorted, as they both grew older. Most of the time he was bossing her around, driving her crazy, and when she would no longer follow his orders, he would resort to violence to get her back onto the track he had chosen for her.

By the time I was working with this family, the violence had become very dangerous, and the police were called to the home to intervene regularly.

This was something that brought him a great deal of shame. The shame made him feel increasingly weak. This made him more angry and the cycle continued.

In the beginning he felt justified behaving this way, because he had told himself it was his job. Only in seeing that this self appointed role is a trick of the mind, could he see that he had become the very thing causing her harm. Peter hated seeing that.

I asked him if he couldn't be in charge, what would he risk feeling? He found whenever he would feel that big love for his sister it would make him feel weak and vulnerable. This is what he was hard wired to avoid. He could see that he had spent his whole life trying to control everyone and everything in order to keep them safe. As he sat with me opening up to all those feelings he began to acclimatise. He realised the feelings didn't kill him. He could allow himself to relax into big love and not do anything. He didn't have to protect or control. Initially, it was really hard for him. With practice he eventually started to get the hang of it.

In the months that followed the old pattern would get triggered often and he literally had to reprogram his reactions to relax, let go, and hand it over. He began Brazilian Jiu-jitsu training with our coaches. This allowed control and strength to be experienced in a healthy way. He learned how to really embrace times of great strength and how to master the feeling of things being out of his control.

Peter stopped being so aggressive at home, he began to relax and enjoy life a lot more. He was happier really caring for his family than when he was trying to be in charge all the time. He told me he had to remind himself "that's not my job" and he would hand it over every time that old instinct arose.

Awareness of this game gave him the power to change. It gave him an option.

In the privacy of your own mind you can discover what happens when you just allow that core feeling you have avoided to be felt. When you allow the feeling of weakness, or terror, or out of control to come and let it pass, you discover more about who you are. You will no longer be stuck and defined by personality games.

Beyond all these games there is something quite huge for you to discover. This discovery will leave you empowered. You need to try it out and experience it for yourself to get it.

I'm still discovering things about myself, my patterns, and who I am. I'm discovering when these personality patterns are interrupted I am strong, safe, real, and powerful beyond anything I could have imagined.

Navigating the Mine Field of Your Mind

It is easy to get completely lost in the mind. You can be sitting; minding your own business and before you know it a thought arises pulling you off in all sorts of directions. That thought stirs emotions and this can continue until you are lost and exhausted. Jacob was a perfect example of this when I began working with him.

Jacob

Jacob was ten-years-old when his parents brought him to me with severe anxiety. This was increasingly causing him problems in his social life, at school and at home. He had started to spiral into a deep depression and a constant state of worry. As I looked at this boy, who was incredibly intelligent and so easy to talk to, I wondered what could have set off these feelings. He shared that his parents had recently separated. This had caused him to feel quite unsettled.

Jacob was a deep thinker, so he tried to think his way out of problems. This is where it all started to go downhill. In an attempt to calm unsettled feelings, he tried to look for safe thoughts in his mind. Going to the mind to feel safe doesn't work because it is the mind's job to protect you by making you afraid, as well as identifying trouble and danger. It is not a great place to come to terms with feelings.

When Jacob referred to his mind, it would cause him to spin into a series of questions like, "what else could go wrong with my family?" He started to picture death, poverty and a lifetime of struggle. His mind was trying to help him by picturing the worst possible scenario, in an attempt to help him plan for it.

This set his body off in a series of constant panic responses, the same way it would if he was in real danger. Parts of the brain can't tell the difference between real and imagined danger.

Jacob had no idea why he was feeling anxious, or even what he was thinking. His only mistake was to follow all the thoughts around in his head looking for solutions. This amplified the nervousness into full-blown fear and made everything feel worse.

Six things happen in your body when you feel anxiety:

1. Nervous feelings get triggered by something.

2. You think that feeling is wrong and it needs fixing.

3. You look to your mind for a solution, causing you to imagine a series of worst case scenario pictures in an attempt to prepare you for anything.

4. Believing those pictures and building on the thoughts lead you to feeling more afraid and anxious.

5. When these feelings increase the body thinks there is real danger. This triggers a part of the brain called your amygdala. It's an almond shaped warrior in your brain programed to protect you.

6. When the amygdala thinks you are in danger it engages your sympathetic nervous system. Your body then releases adrenalin in a fight/flight response shooting chemicals around your body. This is same as when you feel fear. This shot of 'energy' is designed to help you run from anything that could threaten your life, and it gives you a hit of "superpowers". It makes your heart beat faster. Your breathing becomes quick and shallow. You may become sweaty or jittery. It is like a fire alarm going off in your brain. It is literally preparing you to fight or flee into safety. But when the mind looks around and see's there is no real danger it gets very confused.

The cycle continues and if you don't break the cycle it simply refers back to default of looking for a reason to be afraid. The alarm gets stuck. All the while your body is getting overloaded with these chemical reactions making everything feel worse.

What needs to happen to break the cycle is quite simple. Firstly, you need to understand there is nothing wrong with you, your body is doing what it is programed to do. It's natural. To turn the alarm off, you need to make a different choice. It takes some practice, but you can get the hang of it.

Life Hack #7: Get the Mind on Your Side.

In this hack you will learn how to:

- Control the thoughts in your mind that get you down
- Relax yourself, even during stressful times
- Reduce stress and anxiety

Now that you understand what is happening you can choose not to allow the mind to try and resolve feelings for you. Simply, see it for what it is. Don't follow the thoughts. Give these steps a go to get you started;

Step 1: When you notice you are feeling nervous or anxious, interrupt the pattern with one word: "STOP." Then imagine you are pushing the button on a mobile phone and returning back to the home screen. See the thought go blank. Whatever image was playing see it disappear and simply return to a blank home screen. Give your body time to settle. Relax there. Do this as many times as it takes to get it under control, to stay still and quiet, rather than manic in the world of imagination. No matter how convincing those pictures are, it is important to remind yourself those thoughts are not real. Keep coming back to a blank screen.

Step 2: Feel the sensation in your body, and it will pass in a few seconds. It might still feel like fear, or a twitchy or fired up feeling, or it might be really scary for a moment. Let the feelings pass without adding pictures or thoughts.

Step 3: Breathe to switch your alarm off and let your body rest. You will need to change your breathing. Place your hands on your tummy. Start by emptying your lungs - exhale. Using the bottom of your lungs take very slow deep breaths. Watch your hands rise on your belly as you inhale and exhale slowly. By using the bottom of your lungs this way it triggers the parasympathetic nervous system[7] to engage the rest/digest response and releases the stress in your body.

You can do this for about 2 minutes.

With Jacob this worked wonders. He was able to capture his rogue mind from dragging him around all over the place. No matter how convincing the disaster movie he had playing in his mind; it was this simple to stop it and let everything go blank.

---

[7] "AUTONOMIC NERVOUS SYSTEM"

In that blank "home screen" experience he realised that he had just been feeling a bit nervous about the changes in his family. Then he felt those nervous feelings as a sensation, like bubbles in his blood he would report back. Rather than panic in response to this he just relaxed into it. He let it finish in it's own time.

When he was running around in his mind it made him afraid for months. When he just relaxed into it, it passed in just a few short seconds. He was amazed.

For the first time in his life he was no longer afraid of his feelings. He realised they were just sensations that pass and when he relaxed everything relaxed. The thoughts stopped in time, as did all the anxious feelings.

Jacob had flipped his entire relationship with emotions and this will stay with him his whole life. This is emotional resilience like you have never experienced it. There is a power in this that cannot be described, but sure can be experienced.

This exercise and the one below work for every emotion. They work better than all the other strategies you have used to deal with anger, sadness, jealousy, stress, worry and insecurity. Try the exercise yourself with these feelings.

Remember there is nothing wrong with any of your feelings. Feelings don't mean something is wrong or needs to be fixed. Feelings are simply human sensations in your body. Resistance to feelings is what creates a fear of fear itself. Resistance is where humanity's problems and suffering lie. So now is your time to stop.

Change the channel

This little exercise is designed to help you relax your nervous system and quiet the noise in your mind. It works at a physical level, relaxing the sympathetic nervous system. This will help you manage your thoughts, and settle your emotions and stress levels.

Begin by sitting in a quiet space, find a comfortable position. You can even lie down on your bed and close your eyes.

Take a few really deep breaths out then in… until you start to feel you body and muscles relax and soften. Fill your lungs all the way with deep strong belly breathes. You want to allow your lungs to expand all the way. Exhale deeply and slowly through your nose. Inhale deeply through your nose. Exhale deeply again through the nose, gently, slowly, relaxing and expanding the lungs.

Notice your thoughts… imagine it's like you are sitting in front of a television screen, you are holding the remote control. On the remote you have a volume button, and a fade – off button. As various thoughts and mind chatter appear on the screen or come into your mind, one at a time turn the volume button down, until there are no words or sound. Use the fade button to dim the picture until it's completely off…. And then sit still and quiet.

Keep doing this as various sounds, thoughts, memories appear in your mind or on the screen you are imagining. This may take five minutes or so. Take your time. Sometimes there will be nothing left, just quiet and space. Relax and enjoy the quiet space.

When you are ready to open your eyes, just take a gentle deep breath in several times, then open your eyes into the quiet soft space you have created for you.

This is a great exercise to do a few times through the day, or as your morning or evening relaxation. It's wonderful to do before exams or at times your feel stressed or anxious or too busy. I find whatever I am doing comes easier after this, more natural... no struggle. So keep playing with it. Enjoy!

Reinvent Yourself

As you create more awareness of what goes on in your mind - you might be shocked at how you speak to yourself. Now that you have been able to interrupt the patterns of emotions and strategies, are you ready to totally rock your world and change your thoughts entirely? Would it help to silence your niggling self-talk?

Life Hack #8: Fire Your Inner Critic

In this life hack you will learn to stop or change self-talk, but first you have to uncover it. It can be totally life changing to alter what you say to yourself.

Susan

When I first started working on this internal dialogue with sixteen-year-old Susan, who had been suffering anorexia and bulimia for four years, what she discovered was fascinating. This pattern for her was clearly the cause of her struggle with eating. She realised that every moment of every day she was telling herself she was not good enough, not skinny enough, not pretty enough, not together enough as a person, not short enough, not tall enough, not exercising enough, not eating enough, eating too much... and the list went on. All day, every day she piled on the abuse. As you can imagine it left her feeling terrible about herself. She tried to cover up these feelings through either obsessively eating too much or starving herself. Which in turn made her feel guilty. Feeling that guilt she said more terrible things about herself and so the cycle went on.

As she told me the story of her life, it started to become clear where this pattern began. Susan's parents moved from America to Japan when she was very young. Her body started to develop early, when she was eleven-years-old. This was much earlier than her Japanese friends. She was athletic and tall. One afternoon she was standing in the full-length mirrors next to her tiny Japanese friend. Her friend thoughtlessly commented. "You are growing really big and fat." Susan immediately took this on board. She then continued to compare herself to those around her. Instead of appreciating her tall and athletic build, she kept telling herself she was fat and huge. Pretty soon that turned into, "I don't belong. I won't ever fit in, nobody likes me." She started to spiral down. This left her feeling very bad about herself and getting stuck in behaviours she thought would make her feel better, but actually made it much worse.

I saw Susan just a month after we finished working together and she was amazing! Really healthy in her body, learning to love food again, and change her relationship with it. She was really celebrating the changes. After four years of battling with this life threatening condition that had controlled every minute of every day she was finally free.

I've since watched her continue to navigate her way through her natural up's and downs emotionally without slipping back into old behaviours. She has developed a much deeper respect for herself and her body. By continuously changing that self-talk, she keeps turning it into her super power.

Does any of this sound familiar? Do you have an internal critic? I know I do. Maybe it speaks in slightly different ways to you. This is called negative self-talk, vicious words that go around and around getting more and more damaging. Imagine if a friend spoke to you this way. How long would you stay friends? Yet you let this internal dialogue talk to you like this day in, day out. What's the deal?

Now you know several ways to interrupt the patterns of unhelpful thoughts and uncomfortable feelings. The next step is to learn to be kind to your self. You need to replace the negative self-talk with truth. Then you will notice how it makes you feel to speak to yourself better.

VOICE OVER EXERCISE – TAKING CHARGE:

1. Think of situations you find confronting. It might be asking someone out, or meeting new people. It doesn't matter what it is, just pick something that pushes you out of your comfort zone. Notice what you are thinking. Take a moment to listen, and record some of your mind talk below.

2. In that situation what do you hear your inner voice say about you? Does it compare you with others? Does it tell you that you are not good enough? What have you been told that you no longer want to believe?

3. Now write it down. Fill in column one and two ONLY; I've done the first two rows from Susan's exercise to give you and example.

THOUGHT	FEELING	NEW THOUGHT	NEW FEELING	WHAT I REALISED
EG. *I'm fat, I don't belong*	*Sad, heavy, depressed*	*I am good at honouring myself. I love who I am.*	*Lighter, less pressured, more relaxed*	*I confuse myself when I put this pressure on me to fit a mould.*
Your turn:				

4. Now take a minute to close your eyes and notice how your body feels being spoken to this way. Let yourself feel it honestly. You might even like to apologise to yourself out loud. Let your body hear that you are sorry. You just didn't realise what you were doing. It was a mistake.

5. Then imagine in your mind a big campfire, sit around it and warm your feet. Then when you are ready take each of these horrible thoughts, imagine writing them down on bits of paper and imagine throwing them into the warmth of the fire. Keep

doing this until you have imagined all of them being burned on the fire. Feel them leave your body. Promise yourself you will never speak that way about yourself again. Feel yourself receive forgiveness – from you. Feel the relief in your body as you do this.

6. Then invite your favourite person, your hero, even if they are imagined. Ask them to share their wisdom with you. What is the truth? What is the new empowering thought that will fill the space? Listen to them, write it down in the third column in the table above and write how it makes you feel in the fourth column as you hear the truth. Let it in. Allow yourself to believe it. Let these new thoughts be inspiring ones.

7. Then in the fifth column write what you are realising about all this. You can see this in Susan's examples.

8. How will it feel to be living your life with these new beliefs? How does it feel in your body? Imagine how it feels in all areas of your life now without these stumbling blocks, what does that feel like?

Commit to repeating this exercise every week for 3 weeks. Let yourself discover the change in yourself that is possible through this one exercise.

You can also do this with things other people have said to you. It's a wonderful exercise for someone who has been bullied. Be patient with yourself. These are old habits. They have been around for a while and it takes about 21 days to break a habit so that it's no longer automatic.

Celebrate these changes with those around you or in your journal as you notice them. Be kind to yourself as you slip back and forth while you are learning this empowering new skill.

Acceptance, the key to deep happiness...

Happiness isn't just available when everything is going your way. That's easy. We can all experience some kind of satisfaction at those times. It's not this kind of "happiness" I speak of. Deep happiness can be discovered as we truly accept what is happening in life just as it is.

In the few years in my life when things weren't just the way I wanted, without realising I fell into a deep state of appreciating life just as it is. It was a less than perfect life. I parented my beautiful children on my own, in my basic little home, with my bank account fluctuating from empty to less than empty. There were simple moments of bliss in my veggie garden, sweet moments of sadness and flatness from time to time. The water of life became like a still pond where the circumstances around me were just dragonflies dancing over the water, not disturbing the peace. I stopped struggling to get my way, or make things perfect. I relaxed and started to appreciate what was happening. This is the gift of acceptance. Simple acceptance of what is.

When you try to fight what is, you create stress in your body. When you stop trying to resist what is, you are relaxed, grateful for the things you have around you. You can start to participate with life creating visions and goals. You can take action in a way that inspires change. This is a relaxed fun movement. It's not a fight, struggle or effort, it's just a dance.

This also applies to how you view yourself. In any moment you can choose to look in the mirror and pick apart the image staring back. You can choose to look at your face, see freckles and pimples, eyes that are too small, hair that is too curly. You can look at your body and see muscles that aren't big enough, boobs that are too flat and butts that are too big. You can use the ancient torture of comparison to tell yourself you are less than perfect. You can do the same to your life, focussing on all that is missing, the things that are not quite right, all that you don't like and can't accept.

There is a huge liberation in realising there is another choice. You don't have to treat yourself this way. You don't have to look at your body or life and pick them to pieces. You can stop that at any moment. The choice is yours! As you go through this exercise be as honest as you can about where you struggle with acceptance.

Practice Acceptance

What parts of me can't I accept? What do I wish was different?

_____

_____

What do I find hard to accept about my life? My family? My friends? My story?

_____

_____

How does all this make you feel?

_____

_____

Just feel that and keep allowing the feeling until acceptance comes and gets you. Let it all relax....

What would it feel like to simply accept yourself and your life exactly as it is?

_____

_____

How does your body feel as you accept?

_____

_____

What things are you saying to yourself from this place of celebrating your differences and accepting them?

_____

_____

Imagine if everything you are and what is happening is for your good. What if it was all tailor made just for you to experience everything you needed to become all you want to be?

Having No Confidence is Not Really "A Thing"

I often hear these words, I just don't have enough confidence," as an excuse why someone can't or won't do something. I really want to bust this lie open!

Life Hack #9: Confidence doesn't exist without experience.

In this hack you will learn how to:

- Gain more confidence than you ever imagined
- Make your dreams a reality
- Stop making excuses

Confidence comes as you show the courage to get out of your comfort zone even when it's super scary, and give it a go. Don't wait for this visitor called "confidence" before you take action, that's not how it works. The cycle looks more like this:

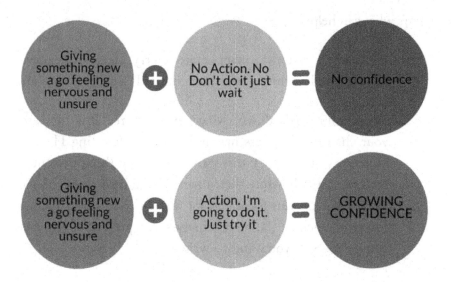

The truth is that the choice is yours. If you choose to take action, to take a leap of faith into the unknown, confidence will be your reward. Chances are you will also grow in ability and that will be a huge confidence boost also. The more times you jump into action the greater your confidence will be in your abilities and most importantly yourself. On the flip side, the more wall staring, and hiding in your phones, hesitating and doubting yourself you choose instead, the more your *lack of confidence* will grow.

Whatever you spend time on and practice – you will become good at. If you practice doubting yourself and hesitating, you become good at that. Or you can practice success until you feel successful. It is all up to you.

Action creates friction, which in turn generates it's own "heat" or energy. This energy can be shared. Remember to "row in boats with like company". Make sure you dance with other action takers. You will be a great support and inspiration to one another.

So did you catch that? Confidence is not just there. It's a heap of leaping into action and putting your self out there, that grows confidence.

Here's what can help…

1. Visualise the result you want before you try. Harness the power of your mind to choose your thoughts and visualise your wins.

2. Write your goals down, whatever they are. This increases your chances of success massively. In an interesting Harvard University study[8] they discovered that only three percent of students actually wrote their financial and career goals down. After ten years this three percent were on average earning ten times as much as the other ninety-seven percent of the class combined. So if you want it - write it down.

3. Make a plan as to what steps are needed, then work your plan.

4. Ask for help. Find the answers you need for the next one or two action steps, then take them

5. Leap! Don't wait for everything to feel right. Don't wait to be ready or for this magic feeling you call confidence. Adrenalin is your body's natural chemical reaction to spring you into action. As it's released in the body it feels exactly like fear. It's not fear. It's a call to action. Your body is helping you move – so just get going. It will feel better as you keep moving towards your goal. Some of the most important things I have done with my life have been the most terrifying.

6. When you fall down, get up. Consistency is half the battle. Don't give up at the first obstacle. Plan for an epic fail. Expect ten setbacks for every victory dance – at least! Failure is a given so get over it.

---

[8] (McCormack)

Did you know that Dr Spencer Silver, the guy who invented Post -It Notes was actually trying to invent a super strong glue and failed. He ended up creating the first "low-tack" glue. His failure resulted in a multi-million dollar idea. Whatever you do, keep trying…. Keep going. We are supposed to make mistakes. It's how we learn. Make some adjustments to the steering but don't slam on the breaks. Can you imagine learning to drive and giving up the first time you found it hard? Learning something new takes time, you have your whole life to master it

7. Be your own coach – give yourself a pep talk all the way "I get it. I can do this. I'm so proud of myself for trying. Let's go." Use your new beliefs about yourself to push yourself forward to a new life.

8. Celebrate every achievement; even the ones that look like backwards steps. Real progress has backward, sideways and forward steps… like dancing. So be prepared to dance your way through your life. Don't leave the dance floor before the song is finished.

9. Stay focused. Wherever you look that is where you will head. So keep your eyes and heart focused forward and that will be the direction you will move. Motivation will peak and dip. You will lose interest some days. Don't wait for that magic thing called motivation either. Don't give in to excuses of why you can't, or why you didn't. Set your plan. Work your plan, no matter what you are feeling. Just take small steps towards your goal every day. Then you will get there. Move anyway, motivation will follow.

10. Remember the best is yet to come. Always see that tomorrow the sun is coming out. You have a fresh opportunity ever day. No matter what yesterday looked like, today is all that matters. So

get up, dust yourself off, redirect if you need to, and leap again. There is no short cut. To grow you must be willing to leap.

So here's your space, write something down... what is the next leap you will take?

_____

_____

_____

When Being Selfish is Awesome

Observe yourself and make a study of you. This is what it is to be awake to be and evolving. You are doing great. Some people take their whole lives to discover how important they are. To focus on yourself and grow as a person is one of the most important investments you can make.

You don't have to accept limitation. You can test it, push it, move it and let your self be limitless. This does take a special kind of person. The kind of person that is willing to look at their patterns and their behaviour to discover what is driving it all and make change.

Life Hack #10: See Yourself As Your Most Valuable Asset and invest wisely.

In this hack you will learn how to:

- Budget your time so you have time for everything
- Make yourself happy, no matter what
- Know what you want and how to create it

Be the REAL thing, don't just talk, walk the walk. The time you invest in yourself now is what you will be good at in a year's time. What are you investing most your time in? Let's put it into a picture so it gets really clear. Fill in the chart make as many sections as you need to account for how you spend your days at the moment – let's look at an average school day.

My 24 Hour Life At The Moment

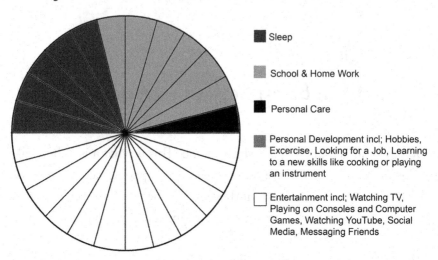

■ Sleep

■ School & Home Work

■ Personal Care

■ Personal Development incl; Hobbies, Excercise, Looking for a Job, Learning to a new skills like cooking or playing an instrument

☐ Entertainment incl; Watching TV, Playing on Consoles and Computer Games, Watching YouTube, Social Media, Messaging Friends

After your eight hours sleeping, seven hours at school, two hours eating and personal care, you have about five hours each day to invest in what you want to be great at. So have an honest look, do you spend the majority of that dressing up for Facebook selfies, or mastering the next level on your newest Xbox game? What you are dedicating your time to is what you are mastering. What will you have to show for it? Success is a collection of the millions of little choices and efforts you put in every day. You become what you invest your time in.

Decide what you want to be – become the hero in your own story. Don't just follow a whole bunch of inspirational stories on YouTube – tell your own story. Become someone you would look up to. It's a decision that you make thousands of times every day that will decide if you are living your life with purpose.

Let's explore:

Who are you? Who do you want to be/choose to be?

_____

_____

What is important to you, what makes you happy? (these are an important key to allocate time to – find or make time for them. They are your 'happy makers' or your values)

_____

_____

Name someone you look up to? What about them do you admire? What do you want others to admire about you?

_____

_____

How will you invest in yourself to make this a reality? What needs to change in your twenty-four hour investment to make this happen for you?

_____

_____

What decisions do you need to make?

_____

_____

_____

_____

Be prepared to make the hard decisions and do the work. For example, if you want others to look up to you for being inspired and successful in your life, is it time to start reinvesting some of your gaming or Facebook hours into achieving this? You could use some of this time getting a job, earning some cash and buying a car. What do you want to create for yourself? What decisions must you make?

_____

_____

How does this feel?

_____

_____

Now let's map out your twenty-four hour investment in yourself. What you are going to change? Fill it in again with what you want your life to be.

My 24 Hour Investment In Me

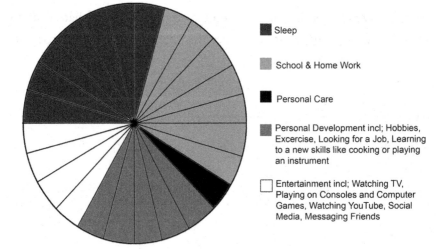

■ Sleep

■ School & Home Work

■ Personal Care

■ Personal Development incl; Hobbies, Excercise, Looking for a Job, Learning to a new skills like cooking or playing an instrument

☐ Entertainment incl; Watching TV, Playing on Consoles and Computer Games, Watching YouTube, Social Media, Messaging Friends

Now it's time to make it happen.

Discover Your Hippie Ritual

Your physical body and how healthy you are, has one of the largest impacts on your emotional wellbeing at all ages.

I found so much happiness discovering the little things that start a day well for me. It took me more than thirty years to discover all of them. So I want to help you discover your magic little ritual and really enjoy it.

For me it goes something like this. Wake up early before everyone else, make my coffee, go walk bare foot in my veggie garden, water and tend to the garden. I pick some greens while listening to my favorite music. I do a crazy dance to get my body moving. I then do fifteen minutes of yoga stretching and then sit quietly to do a visualisation (like the ones in this book) to hush the noise in my mind and focus on my day. After my shower, I make my green smoothie or juice from the garden greens and take my vitamins. I give myself regular "Tam Days" every week where I do whatever I want. This time I use to rest, top up and care for my body whilst also enjoying riding my horse and other hobbies.

These little rituals might not seem like much. But when you find yours and experiment with them, you will see how good they make you feel. Here's some things you might want to include;

- Exercise a few times a week, a walk, get out in the garden, dance like a crazy person around the house, go for a swim... just get the body moving. It really allows the old stale emotions to work their way out of our bodies. Movement and exercise is one of the greatest ways to feel alive, and to get really switched on in your life. It also releases hormones in your brain that literally makes you happier and healthier. If you didn't allow some exercise time in your twenty-four hour investment make sure to add something.

- Get back to nature. Walk in the sand, swim in the sea, grow some veggies, even walk barefoot on the grass. Do something to reconnect with nature. This is critical.

- Diet has a very large part to play in our emotional ups and downs. Sugars, preservatives, processed foods, energy/caffeinated drinks, toxins, all take their toll on your body. Try lay off these things for a few weeks. Replace them with as much raw fruit and vegies as possible. Try combining your greens, a juicy mango and banana in a milkshake once a day. You will be amazed at the difference in your energy levels. This also allows your emotions to balance out and get off the rollercoaster that can be caused by all the artificial stuff. Just give it a try for three weeks. Notice how it feels in your body.

- Do the things you love. Make room for them in your life. For me it's horse riding, dancing, working on my little farm, or yoga. What is it for you?

Write your little morning ritual. How do you like to start the day? Rather than just being dragged out of bed, and forced into it, what could you make your own little morning ritual? It can be anything. If you are into music and dance, it could be a fifteen-minute dance session with some headphones to get you pumped. It can be a run or a walk. My sixteen year-old picks up his skateboard and skates a few times around the block. While it's all quiet and everyone still sleeping, he's gliding around on his board waking up. Then he comes home for a cuppa with me.

Start simple and adjust it as you find "your things." For now, just name three things you would like to introduce into your morning ritual. Even if you have to get up fifteen minutes earlier to do it, I promise it is so worth it.

1.
2.
3.

Life Hack #11: Design Your Life One Goal at a Time

Have you had the experience of setting goals that never happen? Its pretty common and it can be so discouraging. The more times you try a bit and don't succeed, it can leave you less equipped to begin again. This means your intention hasn't been given wings needed to progress into a real vision. This can deflate your determination and shatter your resolve and confidence in the process.

In this hack you will learn how to:

- Set realistic goals
- Make and work a plan
- Enjoy kicking your goals

Imagine a plane trying to take off on a runway full of obstacles – it would be insane, and end in disaster. This is exactly what you do with your goals when you are just vaguely wanting to achieve something but not clearing the runway first. These obstacles are the layers of limiting doubts and beliefs you picked up along the way through life. They won't give your vision a chance to fly.

What Stands in the Way of Your Goal?

At first it doesn't matter what goal you choose. Pick something that feels good for you. Something that is a bit of a stretch that you would like to achieve, and haven't yet been able to. It could be getting the grades you were hoping for, the girl/boyfriend you have had your eye on, the job to save for your first car, giving up a habit you have been struggling with or training for a competition.

Write it down clearly. Paint a wall in your room in blackboard paint and write it up where you can see it or buy window writers and write on your mirror. So you got that… write it down.

Now to discover what your stumbling blocks are you need to ask yourself one of three questions:

1. Do you know what to do?
2. Do you know why you're doing it?
3. Do you know how to do it?

You will need to know all of these areas to move freely forward and achieve your goal. Where there is an obstacle, you will need to brainstorm a solution or ask for help to clear the path.

Answer each of the questions above. Make a plan using what you discover. By approaching your desired outcome in this way, you will burn your obstacles one at a time until your path is clear.

Be Crazy Grateful.

It's from a grateful heart that all good things come. Let yourself experience that, take some time to be grateful for anything. Try and find five things, experiences, people, lessons, anything that you are really grateful for in your life.

1.
2.
3.

4.

5.

Write them down, almost like a thank you letter to life. Take time to really appreciate what you have.

Discover What is Important to You

We are all so different and we value different things. So it's understandable what will make one person feel fulfilled and happy may be different from what will make another person feel the same way. We can only really give about five values our attention at any one time. So rather than set goals and visions around what you think you "should do" or be like, discover a little of your own personal road map to enjoyment.

Make a list of five things that are most important to you. It may be your fitness, family, independence, achieving success, relaxation and friends. Without judging them, just write any top five values down, call them whatever you like. Then next to each one, write three ways you experience these values. Like this:

EG. Freedom: horse riding, working for myself, dancing.

Now it's your turn...

1.

2.

3.

4.

5.

Setting Goals, Seeing Your Vision and Living it

Now that you have cleared what is in the way and you know what is important to you, you can start setting your goals to fully live these values. Your goals will always be on track and be totally achievable now. Now you can really see them take flight because you have done all the ground-work and cleared the run-way. You are ready!

So very simply pick five things that you would like to work on as goals. At the beginning it doesn't matter what they are. As long as they feel related to your values they will feel good to you. Set five goals and write them below. It's a great start to seeing them realised.

1.
2.
3.
4.
5.

Once you have a good picture of what your goals are, have some fun with it. I love creating vision boards. Go pick a bunch of pictures that reflect your goals. Make a poster out of them and write things on it that inspire you. Stick it up where you can see it each day. This process keeps you working towards them. It will also help you to trust life to rush towards you and do the rest. Magic will happen – now you can just enjoy it.

There is so much around us in life we can focus on, so much fear and so much love, so much death and so much life, so much peace and so much war. It has been like this always. You can choose for yourself what your experience will be. Where is your attention? This is your creation. What will you create this week, this month, this year? It's my intention to fly, to be free, to live more and more of my life unlimited by old ideas and experiences. This world really needs you and needs you fully. Living all you can be, no one else can do this for you. This is up to you. What will you create?

Life Hack #12: Be Your Own Cheer Squad

So how do you turn the power of the mind into a full-blown super power? It's much easier now that you know your thoughts, emotions and patterns are capable of shaping your entire life.

In this hack you will learn how to:

- Be your own best friend
- Feel great about yourself and your life

You can now use everything you have learned about emotion, to move all the way through the many layers of emotion, accessing the part of you that is centred, strong and peaceful. I call this your power centre. It's right in the very core of everything you have been trying to avoid.

From here, it is a matter of letting go of all the old ways and thinking that are holding you back. Talk out the things you harbour and let them go. Let go of the beliefs and the limitations. When you are ready consciously choose the beliefs you want about your self and your life. Positively reframe your beliefs by writing them down. Repeat them until they feel entirely true for you. These are called affirmations. Their role is to affirm where you are moving to, how you feel about yourself and your life. Here are some examples:

- "I love my life, I am learning something new every day and I'm grateful to be here"
- "I love my body, I like how I look and I love looking after myself"

- "I am proud of my ability to allow my emotions, stay with them until I access the power centre in the core of them. I am relaxed and clear to move forward"

These affirmations are your creation, so you can totally make them up.

Have a go, and share what you come up with. I always write mine up on a mirror or wall where I get ready. I read them as many times as I can during the day, out loud to myself with embarrassing enthusiasm.

Give it a go, see what happens.

Now LLF - Live Your Life as a Movement

It can take a while to break old habits, to achieve goals you set and to get the hang of all the new tools you have been given. It's very important to celebrate every tiny little change and achievement. Take every excuse for a victory dance. Hey I mean a real live turn the music up, dance around the living room as crazy and pray no one can see your kind of victory dance. Now!

Have champions around you. The five people you spend the most time with, are the people you will become most like. So make sure you pick your tribe well. If your friends are inspiring, motivated and happy with their lives, the time you spend together will lift you up. That's makes your job so much easier. Ask for help when you need it, you know how.

Believe in yourself. If you don't, make your beliefs match what you need to hear until you do believe in yourself. You know how to do all this now. It's ok to be totally full of yourself in a fun way; to know you are amazing, that you can achieve and overcome anything. Believe in you, even if others don't. They are not a reflection of you. What other people think of you is none of your business. Your only task here is to be your own cheer squad - no matter what.

You are now part of one of the most powerful movements on the planet. This is the movement of empowering you. You have found your superpowers – now use them for whatever it is that you want…

See you in the magic my people,

Love Tam

xo

References

1. "Australian Bureau Of Statistics, Australian Government". *Abs.gov. au*. N.p., 2016. Web. 5 Sept. 2016.
2. "AUTONOMIC NERVOUS SYSTEM". *Malonie.com*. N.p., 2016. Web. 5 Sept. 2016.
3. Bays, Brandon. *Journey For Kids*. Element Audio, 2003. Print.
4. Jaxon-Bear, Eli. *From Fixation To Freedom*. Stinson Beach, Calif.: Leela Foundation, 2006. Print.
5. Lovibond, P.F. and S.H. Lovibond. "The Structure Of Negative Emotional States: Comparison Of The Depression Anxiety Stress Scales (DASS) With The Beck Depression And Anxiety Inventories". *Behaviour Research and Therapy* 33.3 (1995): 335-343. Web.
6. McCormack, Mark H. *What They Don't Teach You At Harvard Business School*. Toronto: Bantam Books, 1984. Print.
7. Morgan, Philip and Robert J. Watkinson. "Factors Limiting The Supply And Efficiency Of Nutrient And Oxygen Supplements For The In Situ Biotreatment Of Contaminated Soil And Groundwater". *Water Research* 26.1 (1992): 73-78. Web.
8. Stack, Martin. "Real-Life Economics: Understanding Wealth Creation. Edited By Paul Ekins And Manfred Max-Neef. London:. Routledge, 1992. Pp. Xxi, 460. $85.00; Cloth; $23.00, Paper.". *J. Eco. History* 53.04 (1993): 973-975. Web.

With thanks to all my great teachers for your life's work that influence my potential and our planet.

About the Author

Tamsyn Rose

International Speaker | Facilitator | Author

Tamsyn internationally recognised expert in mental and emotional health. She is the founder of Get Real International, Australia's leading youth and family support organisation for emotional wellbeing and empowerment. For over ten years, she has empowered young people to be healthier and happier. As a mother of five children she applies her own personal wealth of experience to everything she teaches. Tamsyn has been blogging, writing articles, featuring on Television and radio programs for over fifteen years.

This is the first of a series of books ready to inspire real and lasting change in young people, families and the communities they live in.

Tamsyn is also the founder of Choose Life Foundation, a charity dedicated to ending youth suicide in Australia. For details of her events and mentoring programs please go to www.getrealintenational.com

Printed in the United States
By Bookmasters